D1263581

MORE THAN A MEMORY

LITTLE ROCK'S
HISTORIC
QUAPAW
QUARTER

AS DRAWN BY
RICHARD DeSPAIN

TEXT BY
RALPH MEGNA

ROSE PUBLISHING COMPANY
LITTLE ROCK, ARKANSAS

958980

On the cover: The Villa Marre (1321 Scott) is one of Little
Rock's last high style Second Empire Victorian homes.
Restored in 1964 by Jimmy Strawn, Jr., it is now owned by
the Quapaw Quarter Association.

The aerial view of Little Rock on the page opposite
the Preface appears courtesy of the Arkansas Collection
of First National Bank in Little Rock.

TABLE OF CONTENTS

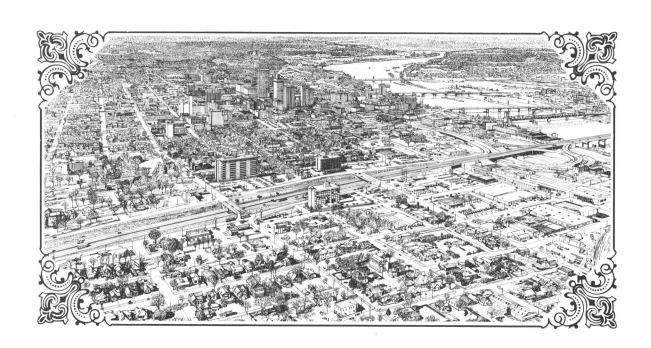

PREFACE

Although greater Little Rock is a city approaching 300,000 in population, the downtown residential area—the Quapaw Quarter—remains the "village of Little Rock." Hundreds of 19th century homes and commercial buildings line its streets, giving the area the appearance of a turn of the century town. The mixture of young and old, black and white, rich and poor are as much a part of its character today as a hundred years ago when people of all types lived together because of the limits imposed by travel on foot or horseback.

Little Rock grew up as a river town and the growth of the city remained near the river, and later near the railroads, until we began to mass produce automobiles. Despite the spread of the city westward, the downtown village held its own until World War II, when it started deteriorating. Then, in a few years beginning in the late 1960s, a new group of urban pioneers reclaimed the heritage that the first wave had established in the late 19th century.

The preservation and restoration of the Quapaw Quarter is one of the great revitalization stories in the nation. There were many demolitions, but enough homes and buildings remain to insure the future integrity of our community's heritage. The village is now filled with children, vegetable gardens, bicycle riders, rehabilitation activity, and new construction—signs of a village optimistic about its future.

This book is an introduction to the beauty and warmth that you can find by walking the streets of our beloved Quapaw Quarter. Come for a visit and experience the historic richness of its restored neighborhoods. The variety of its architecture, its lush green foliage, the fragrances and the feeling of the 19th and early 20th century are yours to enjoy in the village of Little Rock.

PORTER BRIGGS
Publisher and Editor
AMERICAN PRESERVATION MAGAZINE

INTRODUCTION

Though Hernando DeSoto may have visited the Quapaw Quarter in 1541, its first known European guest was Benard de la Harpe, a Frenchman exploring the tributaries of the Mississippi. In 1722, after canoeing north and westward on the Arkansas River some 170 miles, he noted in his journal a "point of rocks" on the south bank. This high ground, the first west of the Mississippi, was already an established encampment for the Quapaw Indians, whose tribal nation spread across southern Arkansas.

Nearly a century later, on the eve of the establishment of the Arkansas Territory, the federal government negotiated a treaty with the Quapaw Indians in which they ceded to the United States all their lands west of the so-called Quapaw Line. This legal boundary ran south from the Arkansas River through present-day downtown Little Rock. In 1824, the territory east of the line was purchased, too.

Little Rock, first the territorial capital and then—in 1836—the new state capital, grew slowly in the years prior to the Civil War. In those antebellum days, the city expanded along the river bank before it pushed south toward the U.S. Arsenal complex, now part of MacArthur Park. Some of the homes built during this period, including Trapnall Hall, the Walters-Curran-Bell House, and the Pike-Fletcher-Terry Mansion, remain important landmarks within the MacArthur Park Historic District.

In the late 19th century, Little Rock experienced a tremendous boom. Its population jumped from 3,700 in 1860 to approximately 40,000 in 1900. Thousands of structures were constructed in the Gilded Age, many of them high-style Victorian homes, churches, and commercial buildings. Elegant neighborhoods, today part of the Governor's Mansion Historic District, were fashioned from the rural countryside south of the city's business district.

Soon after the turn of the century, new residential expansion took place to the west and, by the 1930s, had left the central city altogether. Time and neglect eventually took a toll on Little Rock's once proud downtown neighborhoods and, by the 1950s and 1960s, the urban renewal program was turning many ornate historic buildings into vacant lots.

Beginning with a handful of far-sighted individuals, an effort began in the early 1960s to preserve and restore the architectural heritage of Little Rock. A symbolic step toward this goal was the decision to give the historic area of the city a name. Today, the "Quapaw Quarter" encompasses the nine square miles which constituted the original town of Little Rock and its early additions. Within its informal boundaries there are several historic districts and roughly fifty individual buildings listed on the National Register of Historic Places.

The Quapaw Quarter Association is pleased to have assembled this fine collection of drawings by Richard DeSpain. They illustrate a remarkable success story, the story of a place which has productively preserved its past because people wanted it that way. And it is to those civic-minded individuals and businesses, whose contributions have made the Quapaw Quarter "more than a memory," that this book is dedicated.

LANDMARKS

Every major city has them: the imposing public buildings and great commercial structures, the museums and cultural centers, the churches, the railroad stations, and the schools. The Landmarks. These are places residents and visitors remember because of their size or longevity or purpose. They are to the urban landscape what mountains, rivers, and tall trees are to the natural world. They not only help fix our position in physical space, but in time as well.

The Quapaw Quarter is well endowed with historic landmarks. From the small and restrained Greek Revival buildings at the Arkansas Territorial Restoration to the dramatic modern Gothic sweep of Central High School, the area has sites and sights which remain in everyone's memory. Perhaps no place, though, more embodies the qualities of landmark status than the Pike-Fletcher-Terry Mansion (7th and Rock). Built in 1840, it has been the historic home for three distinguished Arkansas families. The building's quiet antebellum dignity is greatly enhanced by a tree-shaded lawn whose border is marked by an elegant iron fence. It is now owned by the City of Little Rock and used by the Arkansas Arts Center.

11

Begun in 1939, the Arkansas Territorial Restoration (3rd & Scott) is one of Little Rock's oldest preservation projects. Visitors to the Restoration may see four homes which date from Arkansas' territorial and early statehood period, including the Hinderliter Tavern, the Quapaw Quarter's oldest structure, built between 1826 and 1828. Various reconstructed outbuildings, a log cabin, and a reception center are also located on a block and a half site adjacent to the downtown business district.

The Old State House (Markham & Center) was designed by famed Kentucky architect Gideon Shyrock and opened for public use in 1836. Despite some major late 19th century alterations, it has been described as one of the finest surviving examples of Greek Revival architecture in America. Its preservation was assured in 1947 with the creation of the Arkansas Commemorative Commission, which continues to administer the building as a museum of the state's political and social history.

OLD STATE HOUSE

MacArthur Park (9th & Commerce) was originally the site of Little Rock's U.S. Arsenal, established in 1836. Of the more than seventy structures which once comprised the military post, only the 1840 "Tower Building" remains. Birthplace of General Douglas MacArthur in 1880, the arsenal was turned over to the City of Little Rock for a park in 1893. Today, it serves the community as a cultural and recreational center that includes the Museum of Science and History, as well as the Arkansas Arts Center, whose WPA-Moderne style building has been incorporated into a sprawling contemporary complex.

MUSEUM OF FINE ARTS

MacARTHUR PARK: THE ARKANSAS ARTS CENTER

Courthouse architecture was one of America's most important 19th century building forms and Little Rock is graced with two fine examples. The 1881 Post Office and Custom House (2nd & Center), now used by the U.A.L.R. School of Law, is a fine representative of the Renaissance Revival style. Visitors should pay special attention to the exquisite terra cotta details above its third-floor windows. The 1887 Pulaski County Courthouse (2nd & Spring) has lost its clock tower, but may see better days ahead if a far-sighted rehabilitation plan for the Romanesque Revival structure is carried to completion. The 1914 addition, itself a distinguished building, has a spectacular rotunda space complete with gilt trim and stained glass.

The State Capitol Building, opened for use in 1911, was initially designed by architect George R. Mann and completed by Cass Gilbert of New York. It featured six bronze entrance doors made by Tiffany Studios and a 230-foot-high dome. The Governor's Mansion was built in the late 1940s on a Center Street site where the home of Territorial Governor William Fulton once stood. The State Institute for the Blind was constructed on the property in 1870; its over-size bricks were incorporated into the walls of Governor's Mansion. By the 1970s the number of official functions at the residence had grown so great that the state acquired Trapnall Hall, an 1843 Greek Revival building, to use as the Governor's official reception center.

STATE BUILDINGS: ARKANSAS STATE CAPITOL

In the late 19th century, before the arrival of multi-story office buildings, the Quapaw Quarter's skyline was punctuated only by the ornate spires of its principal churches. Among the oldest houses of worship are Saint Andrews Cathedral (7th & Louisiana), built in 1878; the Greek Orthodox Church (8th & Center), first constructed for Winfield Methodist in the 1880s; Trinity Episcopal Cathedral (17th & Spring), whose nave was finished in 1884; and First United Methodist Church (8th & Center), built between 1896 and 1899. The first three were designed in the popular Gothic Revival style; the latter, Romanesque Revival. All feature beautiful stained glass windows and elaborate interior woodwork.

Commerce and transportation have frequently been responsible for the construction of some of the most distinguished buildings in Little Rock. The Capital Hotel (Markham & Louisiana), Arkansas' largest structure with an iron facade, was opened in 1877 as an office building and in 1880 housed President Ulysses S. Grant during his visit to the city. Union Station (Markham & Victory) is the third and most elaborate railroad station on its site since 1873. Today, it is a thriving office, restaurant, and entertainment complex. The Arkansas Gazette Building (3rd & Louisiana), designed by state capitol architect George R. Mann, has been the Classical Revival home of the newspaper since 1908.

Despite their relative youth, several 20th century buildings clearly qualify for landmark status. Central High School (14th and Park), infamous as the site of the 1957 integration crisis, is listed on the National Register of Historic Places as a superb example of modern Gothic architecture. The Al Amin-Scimitar Temple (21st and Main) was designed in 1912 by the firm of Charles L. Thompson; its "Prairie School" style was very avant garde for its day. And the Albert Pike Hotel (7th & Scott), built in the Mediterranean Revival style popular during the 1920s, boasts an ornate lobby with a coffered ceiling and wrought ironwork.

PRIVATE PLACES

While Little Rock has its fair share of museums and historic public buildings, the vast majority of restored structures in the Quapaw Quarter are privately owned and are used for offices, apartments, or single-family homes. Their preservation has made the area a kind of textbook of architectural fashions, since virtually every building style popular in America during the last 150 years has at least one representative. The large number of these historic structures has also made it possible for whole neighborhoods to be returned to their turn-of-the-century appearance, thus creating unique residential and commercial environments.

Because of the building boom during the late 19th century, the Quarter has a great many Victorian homes. Actually a collection of different styles which evolved over a period of forty or fifty years, nearly all Victorian architecture is distinguished by its exuberant form and elaborate detailing. No better example of this building art exists than the Hornibrook House at 22nd and Louisiana. Finished in 1888, its bays, chimneys, turret, and rambling porch are characteristic of the American Queen Anne style.

Built during the decade after the Civil War by the owner of a wholesale drug supply firm, the Lincoln House (7th & Cumberland) was one of Little Rock's finest Reconstruction-era residences.

Among its luxurious appointments were a copper-lined walnut bathtub, crystal chandeliers, and decorative ceiling moldings. Relatively unchanged since its completion in 1878, the house has always been in the possession of the Lincoln family or its relatives. The home is currently used as a private residence and office.

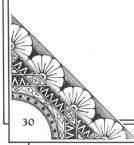

Perhaps the most photographed home in the Quapaw Quarter, Hanger House (1010 Scott), is a stunning example of an American Queen Anne home. Its "moongate" arch entrance and vibrant color scheme are parts of an authentic restoration of its 1889 appearance by owners Charles and Becky Witsell. The house also features operable gas chandeliers, stained glass, and gilt woodwork. It is listed on the National Register of Historic Places.

PRIVATE PLACES: DIBRELL HOUSE

Few private residences in the country can match the meticulous attention to detail exemplified in the restoration of Dibrell House (14th & Spring) by its owner, Carl Miller, Jr. The home has seven porches featuring six distinctly different designs, a forty-five-foot tower, and an elaborately detailed interior. Built in 1892, it was originally the home of Dr. James A. Dibrell, President and Dean of the University of Arkansas Medical Department.

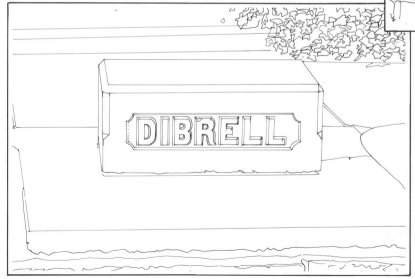

The second Hotze House (17th & Louisiana) was one of the most elegant mansions of its day. Designed by renowned Arkansas architect Charles Thompson in the fashionable Colonial Revival style, it was built directly behind an Italianate cottage Peter Hotze had erected thirty-two years earlier on Main Street. A very prosperous cotton merchant, Hotze spared no expense in the finishing and furnishing of his new home. The house is listed on the National Register of Historic Places.

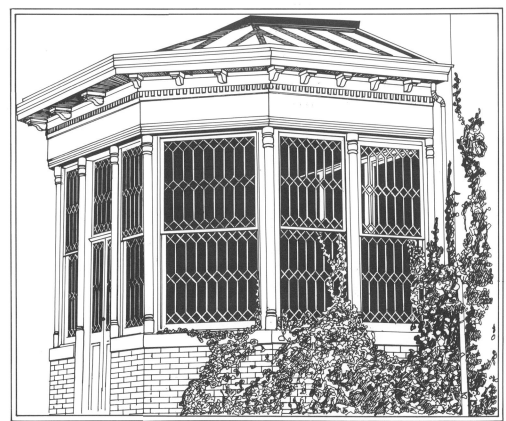

PRIVATE PLACES: SECOND HOTZE HOUSE

Though the Quapaw Quarter is best known for its grand Victorian homes, its essential charm and character come from the presence of hundreds of small, cottage-like houses. Tucked underneath trees and between towering landmarks, the historic cottages recall the lifestyles of the families of modest means. The Jones Cottage (814 Scott), for example, once belonged to a Union soldier who remained in Little Rock after the Civil War. Reigler Cottage (610 Rock) was the home of a baker, and the Bell Cottages (604 East 6th) were rental property attached to the Walters-Curran-Bell House.

COTTAGES: BELL COTTAGE AND REIGLER COTTAGE

GALLERIED ITALIANATE: BAUCUM HOUSE

A gallery—"a roofed passageway above grade projecting from an exterior wall"—was once a popular way to expand the living space of a home using that peculiarly American affectation, the porch. Both Baucum House (201 North Izard), built in 1871, and the Garland-Mitchell House (14th & Scott), built in 1873, are superb examples of the galleried Italianate style. Charter House, constructed in 1879, lacks a real gallery, but attempts to feign one by enclosing the deck above its porch roof.

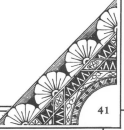

Towers and turrets were important parts of the Victorian design repertoire. Though time and changing fashion have caused the removal of these picturesque details from some buildings, the Quapaw Quarter has many others which remain in excellent condition. Chisum House (1320 Cumberland) retains both its tower and a unique diagonal chimney. The Gans House (1010 West 3rd) not only has double turrets, but is fabricated from stone in a fashion made popular by the great 19th century architect, H. H. Richardson. The sensitive rehabilitation plan for the Holtzman House (512 East 9th) has converted it into apartments which make excellent use of the space inside the building's two turrets.

Because of the abundance of trees in Arkansas, the vast majority of 19th-century homes were of woodframe construction with weatherboard exteriors. Kadel Cottage (417 East 10th), built on the eve of the Civil War, is a good example of an early Victorian building assembled from locally available materials. The Terry-Jung House (1422 Scott) was constructed in 1880 and, except for some missing roof cresting and chimney tops, looks today as it did one hundred years ago. Another well-preserved home is the Reichardt House (1201 Scott). Both its interior and exterior are essentially unchanged from the 1890s.

CLASSICS: GIBB HOUSE

Colonial and Classical Revival architecture swept the nation during the late 1890s and early 1900s. In the Quapaw Quarter, a great many outstanding private residences were designed using these related styles. The Gibb House (1801 Arch), the Halliburton Townhouses (1601 Center), McNair House (1821 Broadway), and Nash House (6th & Rock) are all excellent examples of the turn-of-the-century revival styles. Little Rock architects Frank Gibb, George Mann, and Charles Thompson were all well-known designers whose classically inspired homes and public buildings continue to be productively used today.

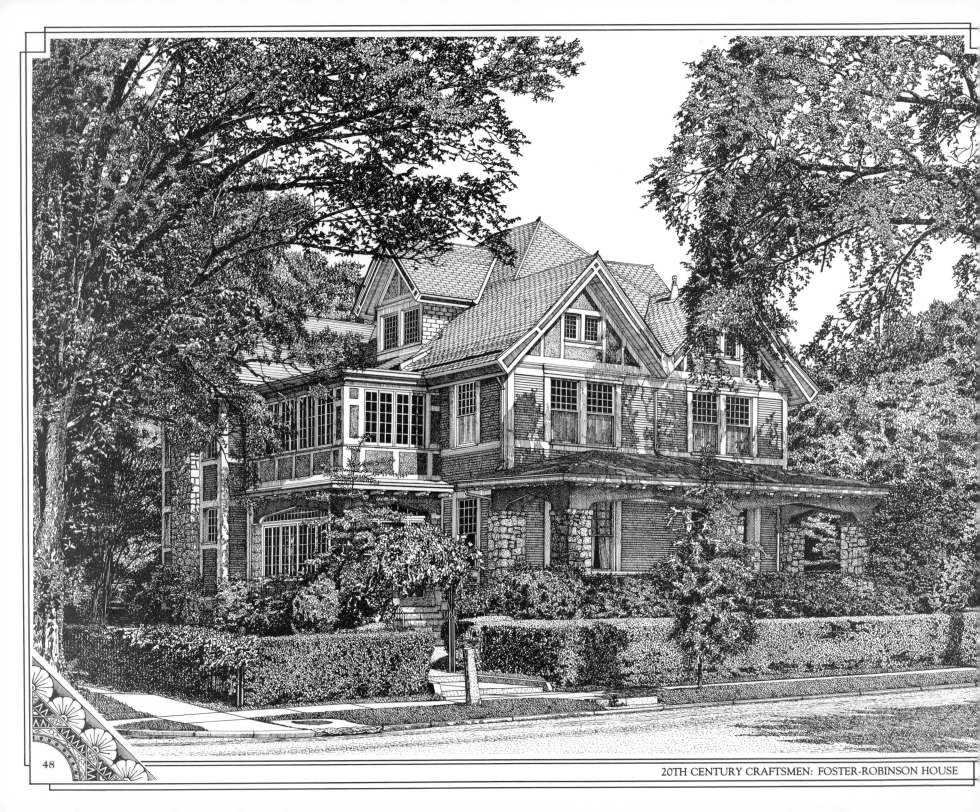

In addition to classical revival architecture, another style popular throughout America during the early 20th century was the Craftsman style. Popularized by a magazine published by designer Gustav Stickley, Craftsman architecture is well represented in the Quapaw Quarter. The Foster-Robinson House (2122 Broadway) is a flamboyant Craftsman home based upon a Victorian floor plan. The Cornish House (1800 Arch) was built in 1919 and has Tudor-style half-timbering. The Bentley House (1223 McAlmont) is a late Craftsman house, now used for offices, which features unusually delicate Gothic Revival detailing.

Through either the fancy of their original builder, or the desires of later owners, a great many buildings in the Quapaw Quarter exhibit split architectural personalities. The Ward-Hays House (1008 West 2nd) was originally an Italianate design which was "up-dated" at the turn of the century with a high style classical porch. The Vinsonhaler House (9th & Commerce), a marvelous 1890s Queen Anne, received similar treatment. The Rozelle-Murphy House (1301 Scott), next door to the Villa Marre, was a Queen Anne residence which received facelifts in both the Colonial Revival and Craftsman styles.

Time and architectural tastes have rendered a handful of homes unique in Little Rock. The Fordyce House (2115 Broadway), an Egyptian Revival residence designed in 1904 by Charles Thompson, has doubtless been one-of-a-kind since its construction. The Wilson House (1020 West 3rd) is one of only a few Carpenter Gothic cottages left in the Quapaw Quarter; at one time, there may have been dozens. The Wait-Newton House (1406 Cantrell Road), more commonly known as the Packet House, can count its Second Empire-style cousins in Little Rock on the fingers of a single hand.

BITS & PIECES

A historic neighborhood isn't just buildings and cobblestone streets. It is composed of a myriad of details which all contribute to sense of place and time. Ironwork, particularly in fences and gates, stonework monuments and markers, and assorted outbuildings are all part of the ambiance which makes the Quapaw Quarter extra special. Unfortunately, though, they are also the items which are most under-appreciated and over-abused.

There are two particularly good places to look for historic bits and pieces. First, examine the yards of some of the most imposing homes. Very often you will find a small shelter over the old cistern, an iron fence in the overgrown bushes, and a carriage house at the rear of the property. Another place to go is Mt. Holly cemetery (12th & Broadway). There, aside from one of America's finest collections of burial markers and monuments, you will find a jewel-like little structure known as the bell house. This Carpenter Gothic building was constructed over one hundred years ago and its bell has tolled the deaths of some of Arkansas' most historic leaders.

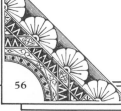

The National Register of Historic Places, the federal government's official listing of America's important sites and structures, does not consider a cemetery eligible for designation unless it "derives its primary importance from graves of persons of transcendent importance, from age, from distinctive design features, or from association with historic events." Mount Holly Cemetery (12th & Broadway), one of the country's few cemeteries listed on the Register, meets all those qualifications. Established approximately 140 years ago, Mount Holly is not only the resting place for Arkansas' historic families, but is also a superb public park filled with an extraordinary collection of stonework and statuary.

In the more than 150 years it has been an established community, Little Rock has acquired a wide variety of sculptures and relics for its museums and parks. The Indian figure in MacArthur Park was carved as a memorial to native Americans. "Lady Baxter," a 19th-century iron cannon, adorns the lawn in front of the Old State House. At the Terry Mansion (7th & Rock), a gazebo and decorative iron fencing are part of an idyllic setting that recalls the home's antebellum and Victorian heritage.

TERRY MANSION GAZEBO AND FENCE DETAILS

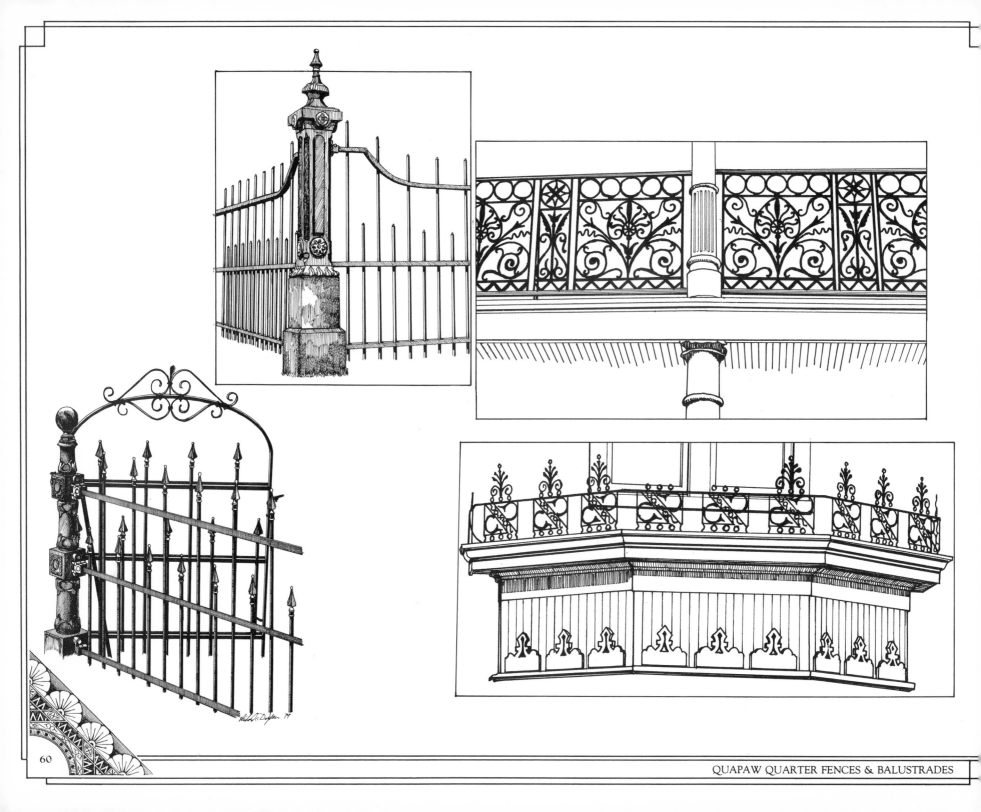

Little Rock's location on the Mississippi Valley trade routes made it very easy for the town's prosperous Victorian families to purchase ornate iron fences, gates, and roof cresting from major companies in places like St. Louis and New Orleans. Though much of the Quapaw Quarter's ironwork was sold as scrap metal in the 20th century, it still appears in remarkable quantities and is making a strong comeback among the restoration-minded property owners. Today, most of the replacement ironwork is ordered from a local foundry specializing in ornamental wrought iron.

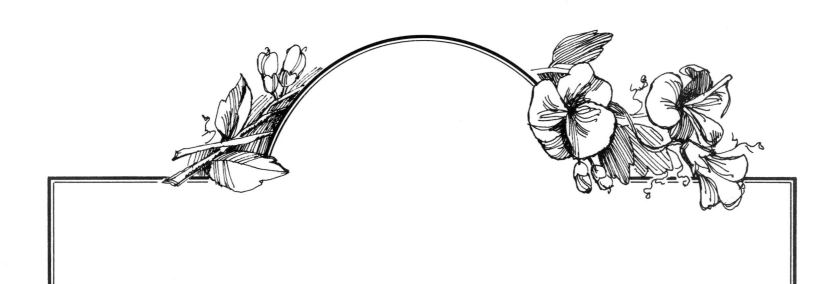

LOST LITTLE ROCK

Sadly, historic preservation in America has been a reactive endeavor. All too often, efforts by citizens to save their local heritage have only come after the destruction of some of the community's best and most beautiful examples of historic architecture. In Little Rock, the destruction caused by the urban renewal program, the expanding need for parking in the downtown commercial district, and the rising cost of maintaining large 19th- and early 20th-century buildings contributed to the creation of the Quapaw Quarter Association and the area's various historic districts.

Long before the losses in the 1950s and 1960s, though, the general improvement of transportation technology and changes in residential patterns forced the disappearance of things like riverboats, trolleys, and downtown schools. And while they, like the Marion and Manning Hotels, are now very much part of the past, it seems safe to say that they continue to survive as more than memories.

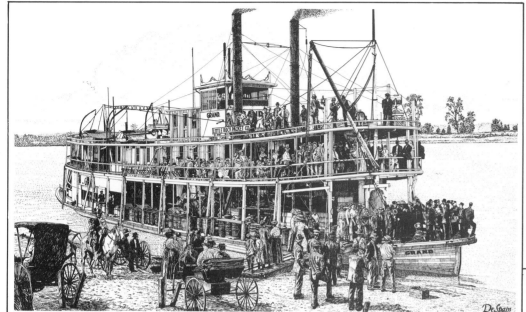

The first riverboat to reach Little Rock was the steam-powered "Eagle," which arrived without advance notice in March of 1822. The visit was followed by the establishment of an important river trade route that served as the principal means of moving passengers and freight in and out of central Arkansas for the next half-century. In the late 1800s, the arrival and expansion of the railroads signaled the temporary end of waterborne commerce. It was not until the 1970s, and the improvement of the Arkansas River channel, that commercial traffic began to increase again and plans were made to improve Little Rock's historic waterfront.

66

LOST LITTLE ROCK: TROLLEY CARS

Little Rock's trolley system, like those in so many other cities, fell victim to America's love affair with the automobile. Before its disappearance, though, the trolley had an enormous impact on where people lived and worked in the city. The routes, which spread throughout the Quapaw Quarter after the establishment of the street car company in 1883, encouraged people to move their residences further and further from the central business district. Finally, in 1904, the trolley tracks headed west and out of downtown altogether; their completion all the way out to Pulaski Heights opened a new era of development for Little Rock.

Like any healthy and progressive town, Little Rock has often found it necessary to destroy old buildings in order to create space for new ones. When, for example, the 1873 train station grew too small for the anticipated passenger traffic, it was torn down for a new, more modern facility in 1911. The Peabody School, located on the site of today's federal office building (700 West Capitol), was a rambling Victorian structure among homes built in a similar style. The Marion Hotel, whose seventy-three years of service to the community came to a spectacular end in 1980 when it and the Grady Manning Hotel were "imploded," has given way to an important new convention complex.

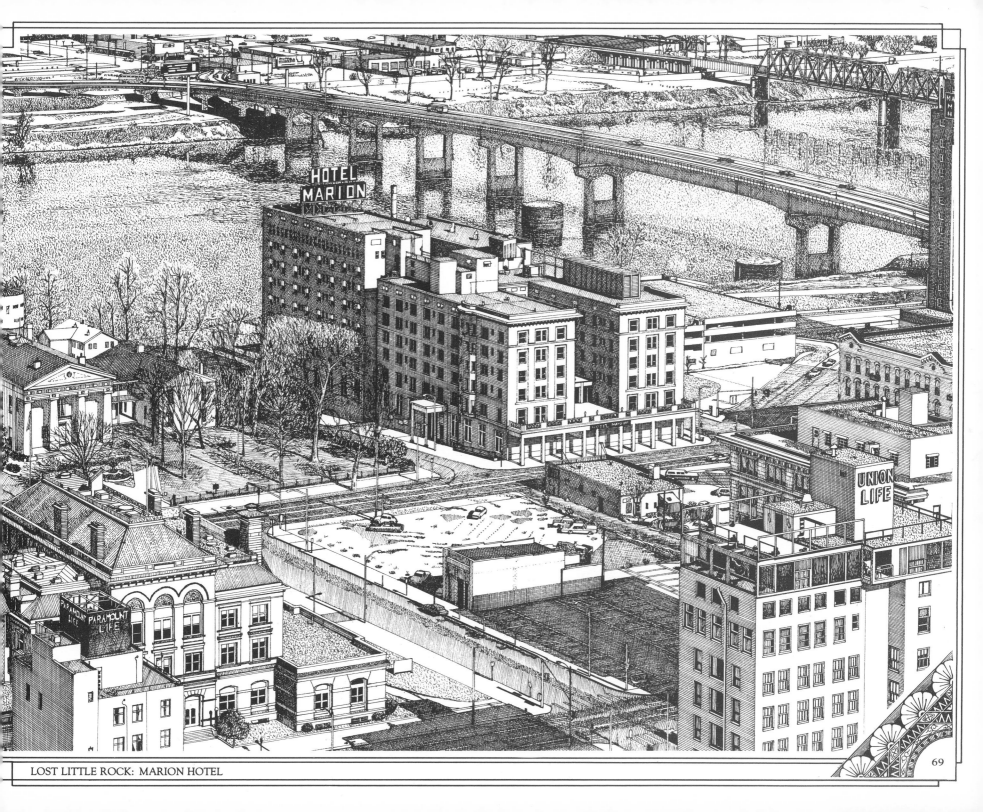

ACKNOWLEDGMENTS

The Quapaw Quarter Association and Rose Publishing deeply appreciate the permission to use privately commissioned drawings in *More Than a Memory*. We would also like to acknowledge the contributions of Designed Communications and its principals, Suzanne Kittrell and Rebecca Rogers Witsell, to the creative design and makeup of this book. Conway Printing Company deserves special thanks for its faithful reproduction of Mr. DeSpain's extraordinarily intricate drawings.

THE ARTIST
RICHARD DeSPAIN

Richard DeSpain is a draftsman by trade and an artist by choice. He has a special love for old buildings which have historical or architectural significance and has devoted much of his leisure time over the last decade to drawing the treasures of the Quapaw Quarter. Mr. DeSpain prefers to work from on-site sketches and photographs, sometimes taking as long as fifty hours to complete a single drawing.

The artist first began drawing seriously while still in his hometown of Blytheville, Arkansas. He studied art as a high school student under Mrs. Alice McManus, a well-known local artist, and later acquired his drafting skills at Burdette Vocational School in Blytheville.